# Arctic Thaw

## The People of the Whale in a Changing Climate

## Peter Lourie

**BOYDS MILLS PRESS**

HONESDALE, PENNSYLVANIA

*For all the children*
—P.L.

# Author's Note

The native Iñupiaq Eskimo people have lived on the North Slope of Alaska for thousands of years. Unlike their relatives in Canada, they accept the term *Eskimo*. In this book, we will use the terms *Native*, *Iñupiaq*, and *Eskimo* interchangeably, recognizing that in Canada the proper term is *Inuit*.

**Iñupiaq** (pl. Iñupiat) A member of a group of the Eskimo people inhabiting northwestern Alaska; also the language of this people. Usage: *Iñupiat* is a plural noun, for example, "The Iñupiat hunt whales in the spring." *Iñupiaq* is either a singular noun or an adjective, for example, "The Iñupiaq sat on the chair." or "The Iñupiaq culture is alive and well today."

We gratefully acknowledge support from the National Science Foundation (Grant No. OPP-0325361).

This book would not be possible without the help of the people of Barrow, among them Alice Brower; Bob Bulger; Richard Glenn; Glenn Sheehan; Craig George; Cyd Hanns; Harold Ivanoff; David Leavitt and his family, especially Lloyd and Jeff; Roy David Ahmaogak; Henry Gueco; and many others in Wainwright and Barrow.

A special thanks to Beverly Hugo, Ben Nageak, Dr. John Reynolds, Jody Shepson, Dr. Matthew Sturm, and Dr. Dana Wetzel.

Photo/illustration credits: Bill Hess, pages 1, 4, 33; Dr. Craig George, pages 11, 19, 20, 30–31, 34, 40; Scientific Visualization Studio, Goddard Space Flight Center, NASA, page 13; Tom Powers, page 17; Dr. Lars Kaleschke, page 28; Dr. Paul Shepson, page 35. All other photographs copyright © 2007 by Peter Lourie.

Boyds Mills Press, Inc.
815 Church Street
Honesdale, Pennsylvania 18431
Printed in China

Library of Congress Cataloging-in-Publication Data

Lourie, Peter.
 Arctic thaw : the people of the whale in a changing climate / Peter Lourie.
  p. cm.
 Includes bibliographical references and index.
 ISBN 978-1-59078-436-5 (hc) • ISBN 978-1-59078-842-4 (pb)
 1. Inupiat—Alaska—Social life and customs. 2. Indigenous peoples—Ecology—Alaska. 3. Human ecology—Alaska. 4. Whaling—Environmental aspects—Alaska. 5. Whales—Ecology—Alaska. 6. Alaska—Social life and customs. 7. Alaska—Environmental conditions. I. Title.
 E99.E7L63 2006
 305.897'1—dc22

                            2006020045

First edition
First Boyds Mills Press paperback edition, 2010
The text of this book is set in 12-point Palatino.

10 9 8 7 6 5 4 3     (hc)
10 9 8 7 6 5 4 3 2 1 (pb)

# CONTENTS

◀ *Whaling boats called umiaqs are made of bearded sealskins stretched over wooden frames.*

# PROLOGUE

*In late April, the snow-covered land and the sea ice blend together into a world of white. The sky is pale with a dusting of flying snow. It is spring in Barrow, Alaska, on the edge of the frozen Arctic Ocean, and something big is about to happen.*

*Any day now, that sheet of jumbled ice over the ocean will crack apart and whales will appear. The Iñupiaq Eskimos will paddle out in their bearded-sealskin boats to hunt the bowhead whales, a tradition the Iñupiat have kept for three thousand years.*

I had heard about global warming, and I wondered what would happen to the native peoples of the Arctic if the polar ice should melt. Would the whales keep coming? Were the hunters already feeling the effects of rising temperatures? Would the other animals that the Iñupiat depend on—the seal, the walrus, and the caribou—disappear? How could native people adapt to a changing climate, and what did this mean for the rest of us? How would we all adapt to a warmer planet?

Because the effects of global warming are greatest at the poles, scientists go to the Arctic to study this phenomenon and to find ways to begin to fix the problem. I made three journeys to the Arctic (in September, February, and April), accompanied by an atmospheric chemist from Purdue University. Dr. Paul "Shep" Shepson put the issue of global warming into perspective for me. Like the Eskimo people we met in the Arctic, Shep was optimistic in the face of some alarming discoveries. In fact, he saw global warming not as some horrific, unavoidable disaster but rather as a scientific and personal challenge.

"Tackling this thing will be the greatest adventure of our time," he said with a big grin.

*◀ When a whale is caught and brought to the edge of the ice, the Iñupiat plant a flag high on the pressure ridge to show others where to come and help with the harvest. (William David Leavitt shown here, April 2005)*

# PART ONE

## Darkness Sets In

### Dr. Paul Shepson

In September on our first trip to the Arctic, we flew an hour and a half north of Fairbanks, a big city in the middle of Alaska. The snowcapped mountains disappeared behind us, and the land flattened out. Finally, Barrow appeared out of nowhere in a vast world of watery tundra.

The northernmost city in the United States, Barrow lies 375 miles (600 kilometers) above the Arctic Circle, on the edge of the Chukchi Sea. Barrow is not a place you can reach by road. Everything must arrive by ship or plane.

There was not a chunk of ice in the gray green sea. A dusting of snow flew across the runway. The pearl sky was cold and raw. Shep and I were like little kids. We were so excited when Alaska Airlines set us down on the North Slope of Alaska, an area encompassing 89,000 square miles.

Shep, I discovered quickly, is a man with boundless energy and a great deal of knowledge about the Arctic. He holds positions in two departments at Purdue University—Earth and Atmospheric Science and Chemistry. He is also the founder and director of the Purdue Climate Change Research Center. His passion for this

*Barrow, Alaska, in September*

9

*Dr. Paul "Shep" Shepson*

seemingly bleak and icy place called the Arctic infuses his every sentence.

Previously, Shep had worked in the Canadian Arctic and in the middle of the Greenland glacier. He had now come to Barrow to help three of his graduate students set up a number of experiments they would conduct this winter. He and I also wanted to learn how climate change might be affecting the indigenous people called the Iñupiat. They have been hunting whales and other Arctic animals for thousands of years. We wanted to talk to them about their culture to understand climate change from a human perspective.

## Barrow

Scientists like Shep have been coming to Barrow to study the Arctic since the mid-nineteenth century, long before science recognized the threat of global climate change. One of those early investigations was to dig down into the year-round frozen earth, called permafrost, to find out how deep it was. It took the diggers two years to dig 37 feet (12 meters). At that time in Barrow the permafrost was 1,000 feet (300 meters) deep in places. Much of the permafrost is still very deep. But because of the warming trend, in summer the surface thaws farther down than before. In fact, some of the underground ice cellars, about 12 feet (4 meters) deep, are beginning to melt. For centuries, the Iñupiat have used these cellars to keep their whale blubber frozen during the summers.

*Iñupiaq hunting for seal*

Wedged between the Beaufort Sea and the Bering Sea, Barrow has about five thousand residents, just over half of whom are Iñupiat. Known traditionally in the Iñupiaq language as *Ukpeagvik*, or "place where the snowy owls are hunted," Barrow is the largest of the eight Iñupiaq communities on the North Slope of Alaska. Here, the Iñupiaq Eskimos still carry on their native traditions and hunt whales, caribou, walrus,

*The Barrow Arctic Science Consortium (BASC), formerly a U.S. Navy base*

seals, moose, and birds. But when we landed, we saw satellite dishes flanking crude box houses painted in many pastel colors. Backyards were jammed with boats, motors, and snowmobiles. Caribou hides were stretched out on racks to dry. It seemed like a strange mixture of modern and ancient life.

Today, the Iñupiat travel on four-wheelers in summer and snowmobiles in winter. Gone are the dogsled days. Eskimos surf the Internet with high-speed satellite connections, yet they also come together to celebrate their traditions. Whales are still at the center of their culture. The Iñupiat believe that when a whale is caught, it has given itself to them as a gift. They are the People of the Whale.

## An Arctic Science Station

Shep and I bunked in scientists' quarters just north of town at the old U.S. Navy base, now the Barrow Arctic Science Consortium—known simply as BASC— a sort of clearinghouse for scientists working in the Arctic. BASC helps scientists conduct their research, and it encourages a two-way transfer of information between scientists and the Iñupiat.

BASC was started by three men, including an Iñupiaq named Richard Glenn. Richard, whose mother left Barrow in 1960, spent summers on the North Slope, then settled here. He is now a whaling co-captain in the tradition of his ancestors.

# The Warming of the Planet

Over a meal of beef and potatoes in the BASC cafeteria, Shep told me his views about global warming. The very first thing I must realize, he said, is that scientists agree—the planet is warming. "There is no uncertainty to this," he said. "What is uncertain is just how fast, and in what manner, these changes are going to occur. That's why scientists make computer models for how it will play out. And these models differ."

What is causing the warming? Evidence points to the greatest source: human activities, especially the emission of carbon dioxide and other gases that trap heat from sunlight. In fact, our activities may not be the only factors that contribute to global climate change, but they play the biggest role. They are also the things we can change.

It stands to reason, Shep said, that what we do on the planet will cause changes in the atmosphere's chemistry and temperature, which in turn will affect our daily lives. "'Atmosphere' seems big, but really the atmosphere of the earth is a very thin layer," he said. "And all of it comes from life on the surface of the planet."

That night Shep and I sat in the cafeteria with three of the ten graduate students who Shep calls "my group." Aubrey Cavender, Adam Keil, and Phil Tackett had come from Indiana to work on their individual experiments to better understand the chemical

*As temperatures rise, the ice cap over the Arctic Ocean has been shrinking. These maps show the change in the minimum ice cover from 1979 (top) to 2002 (bottom).*

interactions between the Arctic Ocean surface, the Arctic snowpack, and the lower atmosphere.

Why are these chemical interactions important? Over the past few decades, the Arctic has been warming up almost twice as fast as the rest of the world. If you want to understand the effects of global climate change, the Arctic is an important place to go.

Shep chose not to dwell on the alarming results of global climate change. Instead, he stayed on the positive track of working to solve the problem. He encouraged me to see how exciting it is for his graduate students to design their own experiments. "These experiments are adventures of their own," he said. "Just think—you build an instrument to measure the tiniest particles of the air. Or you build a big balloon, and you come way up here to the top of the world to fly it. How cool is that!"

Aubrey Cavender, one of Shep's students, was sitting next to us. She was about to conduct this very experiment in order to earn her Ph.D. (doctoral) degree. Nobody had ever flown such a balloon over Barrow before.

*With the help of Iñupiaq people from Barrow, the team used a giant balloon to lift instruments high into the atmosphere.*

## Balloon

It was like a big red whale floating in one of the old hangars of the former navy base. Shep, Aubrey, and I drove out to inspect the monster. It was about 40 feet (12 meters) long and was inflated with helium. Lights on the front and back would allow it to fly in the dark months of winter, and if it got away from the students, it could be destroyed remotely from the ground.

You could see the excitement, the sense of adventure, in Aubrey's face when she talked about the balloon. She was outfitting it to fly the winter skies above Barrow. A sophisticated instrument called a sampler box, mounted under the balloon, would collect samples of air.

"We'll measure temperature and wind speed and take samples of the air at intervals as we let the balloon rise and descend," she said.

Aubrey was eager to get this experiment underway. To collect tiny samples of Arctic air, the preparations had taken years. Shep's other students, Phil and Adam, had also come to Barrow to set up their experiments for measuring various chemical compounds that blow in from the Arctic Ocean.

## Climate Versus Weather

The weather was raw, and the sky was filing-cabinet gray. It was always windy in Barrow, at the top of

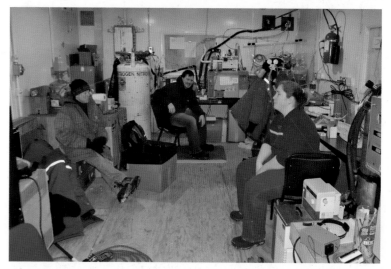

*Members of Dr. Shepson's group used an airplane hangar in Barrow (top) and a small hut on the tundra near the frozen sea (bottom) to conduct experiments.*

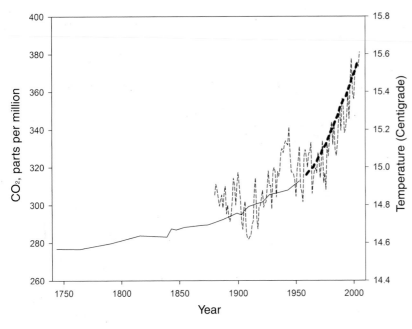

-------- global average temperature in degrees centigrade

------ concentration of $CO_2$ in the air, from measurements at Mauna Loa, Hawaii

———— concentration of $CO_2$ in the air, from studies of air trapped in Antarctic ice

*This graph shows that the amount of carbon dioxide in the air has increased by about 35 percent since the beginning of the Industrial Revolution in the 1700s. Scientists think this rise is occurring because of human activities—the burning of fossil fuels and deforestation. During the same time, the global average surface temperature has increased by about 0.7 degrees centigrade.*

*The data are from the Carbon Dioxide Information Analysis Center, Oak Ridge National Laboratory, and the National Climatic Data Center, National Oceanic & Atmospheric Administration.*

the world. Shep and I walked along the beach where the people hoped the ice would come in soon. Shep said, "My group is interested in *climate*, which is not the same as *weather*. *Weather* is about: Is it cold out today? *Climate* is about the average weather conditions—temperature, rainfall, and so on—over time, like a year or more.

"That's why we study ice and snow," he continued. "Glaciers hide the secrets of the history of the atmosphere. What's cool about ice and snow is that when snow falls down in places like Greenland, it traps the air. If you dig down and pull out that snow, you can measure what was in the air hundreds of years ago.

"What we can see is that, over the past one thousand years, the temperature of the earth's surface was pretty constant until about 1860, the beginning of the Industrial Revolution, when we started burning stuff to make trains go and drive cars and make electric power."

By the end of the twentieth century, the carbon dioxide level had increased by about 30 percent, and Earth's temperature had started to rise. As we have burned more fossil fuels, the temperature has continued to rise.

# The Greenhouse Effect, Good and Bad

Over the past 140 years, the planet has warmed 1.5 degrees Fahrenheit (F), or 0.7 degrees centigrade (C), Shep said. Within the next seventy years it will likely warm another 5 to 10 degrees F (2.8 to 5.5 degrees C). "We're not sure exactly how much it's going to warm and how fast, but we're sure about the warming," he said. Scientists think the warming is caused by an exaggerated greenhouse effect.

"But isn't this so-called greenhouse effect a good thing?" I asked.

Yes, Shep agreed. None of us would be here without the greenhouse effect. The planet is 55 degrees F warmer than it would be without this natural phenomenon.

The *greenhouse effect* refers to the carbon dioxide ($CO_2$), water vapor, and other gases that trap the warmth that radiates from the earth after it has been warmed by the Sun. Greenhouse gases are already in our atmosphere, mostly from the respiration of trees and evaporation of water. Vegetation takes in $CO_2$ and gives off oxygen ($O_2$) when it is growing but emits $CO_2$ during respiration and when it decomposes after death.

The greenhouse effect is a really good thing, Shep said. If we didn't have it, the earth would be too cold to support life.

## Fossil Fuels

"But humans are adding too much $CO_2$," Shep said. By burning fossil fuels such as coal and oil, we convert the carbon in the fuel into $CO_2$, and up it goes.

Right now, the planet is warming above natural levels. This added warmth has many impacts. It changes the water cycle, and thus the rainfall rates, which in turn affects agriculture and all species living on the planet.

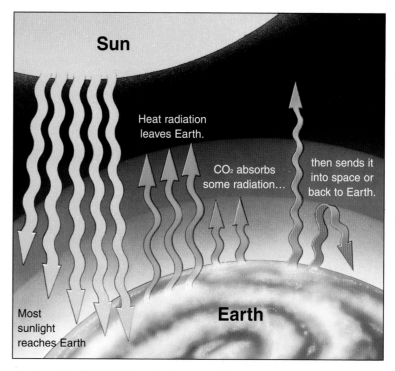

*Carbon dioxide ($CO_2$) and other greenhouse gases trap energy from the Sun as heat. This process is called the greenhouse effect.*

The problem for us today, Shep said, is that the most dangerous thing taking place in our atmosphere—this buildup of greenhouse gases—is going unseen. "Out of sight, out of mind," said Shep. "And we need to have it in our minds in order to comprehend what is happening and then do something about it.

"It's really important to understand why we might not have considered our actions very carefully, and to see what we have done," he said. "How can we know

*A whaling captain and crew maneuver a 40-ton bowhead whale to the shore in Barrow during the fall whaling season.*

what to do differently if we do not understand fully the way we have been doing it until now?"

He pointed out that there are ways to produce electricity without increasing greenhouse gases. Windmills and solar panels can do part of the job, but they have limitations. The most exciting challenge for all of us will be to find long-term solutions.

# Melting Ice

One afternoon, Shep and I drove out to Point Barrow, a narrow bit of land that stretches into the Chukchi Sea. It's the northernmost spit of land in the United States. For many centuries a native community called Nuvuk existed here. But the people from Nuvuk had long ago moved from sod houses into the more modern wood structures in town.

As we drove along the beach, we saw the freshly cleaned carcasses of bowhead whales. It was fall whaling season. During the spring, the Iñupiat must go out sometimes miles onto the ice to hunt whales. But in the fall, the whales are hunted from motorboats on the open water.

Just the day before, whalers had brought in three

huge whales. Friends and family had come from town to help harvest the whales, and now the only things left standing in the raw, gray light were their spines, picked clean. The Iñupiat depend on the whole whale. They use almost every single part, much as the Plains Indians used bison years ago.

We heard that the Iñupiaq whale hunters were taking their motorboats farther and farther out to sea each year to hunt the bowhead whale in the fall, when the whales swim southwest from the Beaufort Sea to their wintering areas in the Bering Sea. We also learned that the Iñupiat are raised to treat others, especially elders, with respect. When someone catches a whale or any animal, the hunter shares it with relatives and elders and the community. From an early age Iñupiaq children are taught to be generous. I thought that maybe one of the reasons we were in this global warming situation was because so many of us are selfish. We buy big, gas-guzzling vehicles, we crank up the heat in winter, and we rarely think of the consequences for other people.

Shep and I parked in front of the ocean. Shep shook his head. He said, "The effect of the warming planet is felt way up here, yet the people in this region did nothing to cause it. They are only the recipients of our folly."

Fifteen to 20 percent of Arctic sea ice has disappeared in the past thirty years, he said. And the Arctic is losing its ice faster and faster.

"Ice normally reflects about 90 percent of the sunlight that strikes it," he said. "But if the ice melts and leaves us with water, the open ocean absorbs about 80 to 90 percent of the light that strikes it. Light that is absorbed is converted into heat.

"This warms the surface and thus the atmosphere. As the atmosphere warms, it melts even more sea ice. As the sea ice melts, more of the incoming solar radiation is absorbed by the oceans, which warms the oceans and thus the atmosphere, which melts more ice, and so on. This is called a positive feedback."

*The polar bear hunts from the ice on the sea.*

*The snowy owl feeds on lemmings.*

This process may not go completely unchecked. Just as positive feedbacks increase global warming, negative feedbacks decrease it. For example, as higher temperatures melt sea ice, they also evaporate water. That airborne water can form more clouds, which reflect sunlight. So clouds may decrease the amount of warming. But how much? No one knows.

"Polar bears and seals and foxes and little lemmings run around on the ice," Shep continued. "The polar bears need the ice to sneak up on the seals that live under the ice. Take away that ice, and the seals won't be able to hide from the bears. So we could lose some fascinating and important creatures if the polar ice cap melts."

Some scientific models of global-scale climate change currently predict that by the end of this century, the Arctic Ocean will be ice free in summer. The complete loss of sea ice may spell doom for several Arctic animals. Polar bears use the ice as a platform for traveling, feeding, denning with their cubs, and reaching open water. Ice seals also need the ice for rearing their pups. And bowheads escape predators such as orcas by staying under the ice where such predators cannot live.

The Iñupiat stand to lose a great deal. The animals on which they depend will disappear or retreat to other areas, and their culture will change forever. I wondered, could it survive such changes?

One bleak sign for the Iñupiat is that wealthy nations might actually receive a few benefits from an ice-free Arctic. If glaciers were to melt away, rising sea levels would flood coastal areas worldwide. But at the same time, an unblocked ocean at the top of the world would then open new fishing areas and shorter shipping routes.

## Wainwright

One day Aubrey, Shep, and I flew an hour down the coast to a little whaling village of five hundred Iñupiat. Wainwright, like Barrow, has no roads leading in or out. You can get here only by boat or plane. The people we met were warm and friendly. In the town hall, Roy David Ahmaogak told us that many changes were happening here. More and more hunters were falling through the thinning ice. Seals were harder to find. People were fishing more often as the waters remained open for longer periods during the year.

One man in the office smiled and said with surprising optimism, "Heck, if there's no more ice and polar bears can't be on the ice, they'll go inland. They will survive. And if it means more fishing, we'll get more fish." He believed in the Iñupiat's ability to adapt.

Roy told us that many residents of Wainwright would be dancing at a big Iñupiaq festival in February, when all the villages come together to celebrate the successful whaling season. He invited us to come back to see it.

*Jay Lee Peetook gave me a carving of whale flukes that he had made from baleen, the hard material that bowhead whales use to strain their food from seawater.*

*The green house is the home of Ben Ahmaogak, a well-known whaling captain.*

*Where the tundra meets the sea*

21

# PART TWO

# Cold and Dark

## Onto the Ice

THE EARLY FEBRUARY SUN ROSE LOW INTO THE SKY for only about five or six hours a day. When it disappeared, everything became dark and cold with constant strong winds buffeting the snow in our faces. The temperatures stayed below zero for days, sometimes dropping to 60 below with the wind chill. February's cold made me happy. It didn't feel as if global warming could ever come to this deep-freezing place.

During the twilight, Shep and I walked out on the ice for the first time. Keith Williams, an Iñupiaq from BASC, came with us to protect us against bears. He carried a gun and kept a wary eye out as we stumbled onto the frozen ocean.

We asked what the whalers were doing during this season. Keith had been whaling many times. He said that the Iñupiaq women were sewing bearded sealskins together to make *umiaqs (OO-mee-acks)*, the traditional whale-hunting boats. The men were preparing their harpoons for the spring whales. There were still three months until ice breakup, but one old man in town had said to me earlier that day, "I can

*Dr. Shepson and Keith Williams*

*smell* the whales. All I can think about is getting out on the ice and getting whales."

Keith kept kicking at the snow to get a better idea of what was happening to the ice. He was looking for cracks.

Keith's face had the faraway look of a sea captain as we walked over the ridges of ice. He stopped, gazed out at the vast whiteness, and walked cautiously onward. Sometimes he would stop and gaze in silence at the horizon for a very long time. Then he said, "Bears can hide behind anything. You can walk straight up to them with-in a few feet and not even know they're there." He had no hatred for bears, just respect.

## Kivgiq

That February Shep and I spent many hours in the high school gymnasium, entranced by the Iñupiaq celebration of Kivgiq (KIV-ee-ak). Known also as the Messenger Feast, Kivgiq takes place in the heart of winter every few years, during this time of darkness

*Dancing at Kivgiq in the high school gym*

*Roy David Ahmaogak*

and cold. To honor the Iñupiaq whaling tradition, Kivgiq brings all the people of the North Slope, from each of the eight communities, together to share stories through dance, drumming, and song.

Kivgiq is sponsored by the *Umialgich*, (OO-mee-ahl-gich), the leaders of the communities, usually the whaling captains. These well-respected Umialgich send out two messengers, called *Aqpaqsruqtit* (ahk-pahk-FROOK-deet). The messengers bear gifts and food to other Umialgich in other communities, asking them to come celebrate together.

*Ernie Frankson of Point Hope*

Kivgiq opened with a short foot race by young men through the streets of Barrow to the school gym. A seal-oil lamp was ceremonially lit, and the drummers and singers from the different villages lined up on the bleachers. In fact, for three whole days and nights, villagers came to sing and dance and drum.

Roy Ahmaogak and the Wainwright dancers were here. Bands from each village took turns playing while individuals acted out stories in dance and chants. The drumming was hypnotic.

I saw more laughter in these three days than I had seen in years. It was particularly thrilling to see the whaling captains as they were called down from the stands to dance together. Then all who wanted to dance were invited to do so, and the gym floor grew crowded with young and old alike.

## Chemistry in the Air

Aubrey had been having trouble launching her balloon on account of the constant high winds. Without getting the balloon into the air, she could not collect the samples she needed. But on those days when the wind died, she had lots of help from the Iñupiat from Barrow, and she was happy to get the balloon high above the town. Phil Tackett had begun to analyze her samples, and he was getting the data he needed.

We visited Shep's other grad student, Adam Keil, who was studying highly reactive elements called

*Kivgiq drummers and dancers from Point Hope (above) and Wainwright (below)*

*Aubrey Cavender stands on top of the snow-covered hut.*

halogens. People use one kind of halogen, chlorine, to kill germs and break down chemicals that form stains in laundry. In the Arctic Ocean, halogens arise naturally from sea salt as it lies on sea ice. Halogens play many roles in the Arctic air. Scientists think they help clean the atmosphere of pollutants. Adam was working to understand what might happen if there was no sea ice to help launch halogens into the air.

Every day he would either drive the pickup or take his snowmobile across the tundra up the coast to the little cabin he and Aubrey had established as a mobile lab. Here he would capture samples of air from the Arctic Ocean, untainted by any industry, and then he'd run these samples through instruments that tested for chemicals like halogens and ozone.

*Phil Tackett examines data at BASC.*

*Adam Keil takes a break from his instruments inside the hut.*

*Salty ice crystals called frost flowers grow on new sea ice. Scientists think frost flowers help important chemicals, including halogens, rise into the air.*

Ozone, I learned, plays several roles—some helpful, some harmful. In the upper atmosphere, a layer of ozone plays a helpful role as the original sunscreen. The "ozone layer" blocks out most of the Sun's harmful ultraviolet rays. (Pollutants have reduced the amount of ozone up there, and some chemicals have been banned to let the ozone layer repair itself, which is happening.)

In the lower atmosphere, ozone can play different roles. In small amounts, it helps clean the air. But too much ozone can be a pollutant. It is harmful to all living things. And it is a greenhouse gas.

"The atmosphere is in a delicate balance," Shep said. "We need some ozone, but not too much."

Before I left, I came across a man who was gunning his snowmobile right up over a road. Perhaps he was just killing time before the ice broke up and the hunt began. Over and over again, he raced his snowmobile up a slope to the road, then flew upward so high he cleared the ground by five or six feet. He had a friend with him to watch for traffic, not that there are many cars in Barrow.

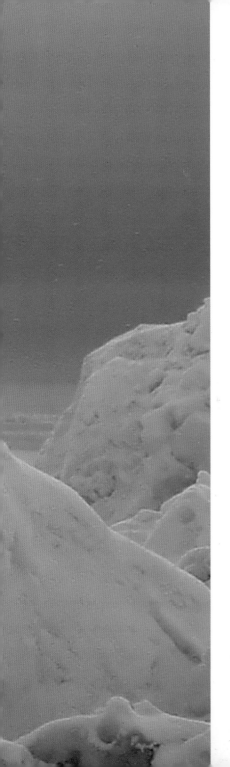

# PART THREE

## Light Returns

### The Coming of the Whales

It is late April on our third trip to Barrow, a windy 0 degrees Fahrenheit (-18 centigrade), and we are standing where the snow-covered land meets the ice. What is different from when we were here in February is that now the Sun is up most of the day and "night." Looking out from land to where the polar bears are hunting for seals, we can see the ocean covered in a textured sheet of crazy, jumbled ice called a pressure ridge. For more than a month the whaling crews have labored to make snowmobile trails through this chaotic pressure ridge, so that when the ice actually opens, there will be a way to get people out to help harvest the whales and to get the whale meat and blubber back to town.

The Iñupiat have never overhunted the whales or any other Arctic animal. They take only as many animals as they need to feed themselves, and they use every part of each animal that they take. For all eight villages, some seven thousand Iñupiat, only about forty-five bowhead whales are taken every year.

◀ *Sunrise in early May*

*An Iñupiaq whale hunter tows an umiaq over the ice to open water.*

Scientists estimate that there are now about ten thousand bowhead in Arctic waters, and the population is healthy and increasing. There may have been as many as twenty thousand whales before commercial fishermen came from Nantucket and New Bedford, Massachusetts, to hunt them in the last half of the nineteenth century. That whaling industry nearly brought the bowhead to extinction. In 1910, when commercial whaling came to an end, there may have been no more than one hundred bowhead left. Since then, only the Iñupiat have been harvesting them, and the bowhead population has recovered nicely.

As we stand at the edge of the ice, we can see whaling crews dragging sleds with sealskin umiaqs and whaling equipment out to the whaling camps on the frozen sea. This process goes on for days and, with so much light, well into the night. For now, the easterly winds are favorable for the ice opening up soon. There is a thrill in the air as the whaling captains and their crews move from their homes to their camps on the ice. Many will stay out there for the whaling season, perhaps a month or more.

# David Leavitt Sr. and Crew

On the plane flying in from Fairbanks, I had sat with a man who did not speak to me until the last ten minutes of our flight. He became very excited when he saw the ice around Barrow. The man said, "Look at that." He pointed to a mile-long crack in the ice, where he thought perhaps the open water would first form in a few days.

His name was Lloyd Leavitt. He invited me to his house to meet his father, David Leavitt Sr., a well-known whaling captain and a respected Iñupiaq elder.

The following Sunday I went to Lloyd's house after he and his family came back from church. I walked through the garage, which had been transformed into a whaling workshop. Lloyd's brother Jeffrey showed me his harpoons, and I felt as if I'd stepped backward in time to the days of commercial whaling. In fact, much of the equipment being used today is similar to the equipment of a hundred years ago.

When I stepped into the house, I was greeted by a kind-looking elderly man. David Leavitt had grown up in a small village east of Barrow. He moved to Barrow in 1943, when only a few hundred people lived here. Lloyd's father had been sick recently and probably would not participate in the spring hunt.

Over a bowl of caribou soup, I listened to David's voice, his English heavy with Iñupiaq sounds. We sat around the kitchen table, the extended family all talking and eating frozen chunks of whale blubber, or *maktak*. This blubber still had black skin attached, more than an inch thick.

With a sharp hunting knife, David shaved slivers from these frozen blocks of blubber and skin. He looked happy. Sometimes he dipped his blubber in seal oil.

He offered me some of the maktak. It was quite fishy tasting, but good.

He said that whale hunts in the spring have become more dangerous than in previous years. He thought this was probably due to global warming.

David's worry is a tough one. The evidence of global climate change is in average changes over large regions. It is hard to show that global warming was the

*Iñupiat hunting bowhead*

*Whaling captains from Kaktovik*

*During the spring whaling season, Iñupiaq whalers go out to where the water opens. These sections of open water are called leads.*

cause of any local event. But even if the increasing dangers on the ice are due to local weather changes, they show what the Iñupiat hunters will face as global warming increases.

The dangers lie in shore-fast sea ice. This ice does not move with the currents. Instead, it is connected, or "fast," to the shore and extends over the water. When some of the sea ice breaks up, opening up areas where whales can swim, the hunters go across the shorefast ice to hunt.

Now the shore-fast ice had become less stable. Scientists are studying this phenomenon, Lloyd said. But while they study it, certain years have brought near disaster for the whalers. Sometimes whalers have

been stranded on sheets of ice that break away and begin to float out to sea. The whalers then must be rescued by helicopter. Again, this increase in strandings may or may not be due to global warming today. They certainly paint a grim picture of the future.

On every trip to Barrow, I found the Iñupiaq people, like the Leavitt family, generous and full of good humor. There seems to be a need for generosity and goodwill in the Arctic, perhaps because there is a better chance for survival if people work together. Or maybe it's because the whale is the center of their culture and it takes a whole village to bring in one of these enormous mammals.

The Iñupiat catch fish and hunt many other animals, such as caribou in the fall, seals and walrus in the spring and summer, and many birds. But it is the whale that brings together the whole culture and the eight villages on the North Slope of Alaska.

## Dogsled Like the Old Days

One day I went out on the ice with dogs, the way the Iñupiat used to harvest whales. Before the arrival of the snowmobile in the 1960s and early '70s, dogs and sleds were the only means of transportation in the winter.

My friend, biologist Craig George, took me a few miles out onto the ice to a place where the very next day the ice broke up and the whales came swimming by. It was thrilling to travel so silently, following the

rough trails in the pressure ridge that the whaling crews had cut through the jumbled blocks of ice. The dogs' feet churned up the cobblestones of cut ice, and the sled sizzled along the twisted trail.

Out with the dogs that day, I began to see the magic of ice. It's all about being out on the ice. Reading the ice. Knowing the ice firsthand, knowing it from your grandfather, your uncle, knowing it in your genes. Scraping it with a foot and digging a hole through it to let down a weight to know its depth. All the signs ice can give. What's happening at the edges of the ice floe, the size of the floes, whether it's multi-year or first-year ice. Everything matters when you're out on the ice.

It's all about the ice. And the feelings you get out there. My gosh, the feelings are intense!

*Whale biologist Craig George readies the sled dogs, then enjoys the traditional mode of travel on the ice, a mile from shore.*

*Richard Glenn and his wife, Arlene*

# Richard Glenn

I wanted to meet the man who had helped start BASC, a man who was striving to bring scientists together with native people in an effort to have these two groups share information.

Richard Glenn was sitting at his computer in his office in Barrow. He looked tired but happy. He was a whaling co-captain himself and he and his crew had been cutting a trail for long hours many miles south of Barrow, where he had a hunch the water would open first. Open water is called a lead.

He said, "Tomorrow or the next day the ice should all open up. Tomorrow we're going to learn where the leads will be. Everyone knows we're almost there. On Monday, you're going to see people who don't want to go to work. They'll go whaling."

He pointed to his screen and said, "This is near-real-time ice imagery, something called Synthetic Aperture Radar." The satellite image he was showing me had been taken through clouds. Pictures of the ice from space could be photographed night or day. Whaling captains like Richard could zoom in on parts of the ice they might be interested in. Richard studied these photos now to decide where the edge would break so he could begin to build his camp as close to shore as possible, but also close to where the open water would be. Very tricky stuff.

"This high-tech image," he said, "is more like hindsight for us. The images help us know more about what we already saw out there in person." Satellite photos were now being used in conjunction with traditional knowledge that has always come from actual observations by the experts—the elders.

"If the elders tell me I'm going to float away on that piece of ice and that I should stay clear, well, then I trust them," he said. "Ignoring information encoded in the culture can kill."

I asked about global warming and how it might be affecting the ice. Shep and I had read reports that in the past ten years an increasing number of whaling crews were getting stranded by unstable ice. Was global warming the cause?

Richard Glenn paused before answering. He said,

*Richard Glenn studies a satellite image of cracking sea ice to plan a whale hunt.*

*Bowhead whales breathe air at the surface of the water through two blowholes.*

"Maybe I'm trying to avoid the truth, but I don't think this is necessarily the result of climate but rather the result of weather. It's the result of a few weeks of conditions, and it's a toss of the coin every day."

Later, Richard told me that he's had a recurring dream recently about catching whales in shallow water, right off the Barrow shore. He also said his sight was going bad and that he now relies on his harpooner to describe the ice out there before he makes any decision.

I said, "Richard, that means you rely totally on someone else."

He replied, "That's what life is all about."

# First Whale

Richard Glenn was right. The very next day, the chatter on the radio increased all morning. Then a voice crackled on the air waves, "They got a whale. It's the David Leavitt crew. They got one." And so began the spring whaling season—just one more season in a series of thousands and thousands of spring seasons for as far back as Iñupiaq oral history goes. And then even before that.

Men and women and children were now racing out on the ice to help bring in the whale. It takes much more than one crew to haul a whale onto the ice and harvest it.

I found myself also gunning my snowmobile on the narrow and treacherous trail through the blocks of sea ice where only yesterday I had taken the dogsled.

*Heading out on the ice to the whales*

*The Iñupiat use straps or ropes to pull each whale out of the water for harvesting.*

I followed three whale biologists who wanted to take measurements and samples of the whale for study. We rode about a mile out and came across many snow-mobiles already there.

A rope was tied to the flukes of the whale near where the ice met the deep blue of open water. It was a sunny and unusually mild day for late April. During a previous whale catch on this same day years before, it had been 60 degrees colder. The mildness of today, in fact, worried me. What if this unusually warm day was not the result of weather but rather of climate change?

Lloyd Leavitt and his family were cutting a hole in the ice to set up the block and tackle, so all of us could get on the ropes and haul up the whale. It was a small whale. About fifty of us started pulling on the rope. Some whales weighing as much as 60 tons

*The whale harvest is a time when people come together to work and share their traditions.*

*Lloyd Leavitt describes how he caught his whale.*

could take two days to haul up, but this one took hardly an hour.

Lloyd, I could see, was happy. And I was thrilled that he was the one to get the first whale of the season. His family cooked some of the blubber, and when I was given my share I gobbled it up, warm and like fishy butter.

As men and women began to distribute large slabs of blubber, I looked out to sea. Other whales were surfacing and blowing steamy air into the cool bright day. It was so warm that I had to take off my heavy winter jacket.

For the next five hours, friends and family from Barrow worked together to harvest this 10-ton whale the

*The Iñupiat use almost every part of the whale, dividing it into equal shares.*

Gathering for the harvest

Cutting sections of blubber, or maktak, an important part of the Iñupiaq diet

Cutting and peeling away the maktak

way whales have been harvested for what seems like forever—everyone laughing and working in unison, some cutting, some pulling, some distributing slabs of meat.

And I thought how tragic it would be if after so many millennia, the ice disappeared and this spring scene, a ritual at the center of a whole culture, were to stop—if the Iñupiat ended up eating Big Macs instead of the whale meat and blubber that give them all the nutrients they need in this harsh environment. But most of all, it seemed terribly wrong that they might lose the very thing that holds their culture together— the pursuit of the animals they love and need, all because the rest of us living thousands of miles away are unwilling to meet the challenge of global warming.

*Shares of maktak*

*Plates of tough baleen, used to make many things, such as boats, baskets, and nets*

# EPILOGUE

**W**HEN I LEFT BARROW FOR THE LAST TIME, I decided to change my own ways. I wanted to celebrate the natural world and the people who still live in the Arctic. To accomplish this, I realized I must change my own bad habits. Just because I can't see those greenhouse gases that come from my fossil-fuel-burning SUV and from all the lights I leave on when I'm not in a room, that doesn't mean the gases aren't there. Or that they are not dangerously building up in the atmosphere.

I am committed to changing. The poet John Donne was right when he said that no man is an island, that we are all connected.

Shep had helped immensely. Turning the tide on global warming would become my personal challenge, too. He and I had gone to the Arctic, and we had seen what could be lost if we do not meet the challenge.

Shep is right. To keep the planet safe will be difficult but not impossible. And it will surely be one of the greatest adventures of all our lives.

◀ *The David Leavitt crew and family pause for a photograph before everyone begins the harvest.*

# GLOSSARY

**Aqpaqsruqti** (plural: Aqpaqsruqtit) – Iñupiaq term for a runner or messenger.

**atmosphere** – the envelope of gases surrounding Earth.

**baleen** – a series of thin, hard strips that grow in place of teeth from the upper jaws of bowhead whales, gray whales, and other species, all known as baleen whales. The whales use baleen to strain their food—small creatures called krill—from seawater.

**blubber** – the fat of sea mammals, especially whales and seals.

**bowhead whale** – a black whale that lives in Arctic seas and feeds by using its baleen to skim plankton and krill from the surface of the water.

**carbon dioxide (CO$_2$)** – a colorless, odorless gas produced by burning fuels, by decay, and by respiration of vegetation. It is a powerful greenhouse gas and is removed from the air by plants in photosynthesis.

**climate** – the average weather conditions (temperature, winds, precipitation) over years for a particular region and time period.

**Eskimo** – a native inhabitant of the seacoasts of the Arctic and sub-Arctic regions of North America and the northeastern tip of Siberia. The Iñupiat accept the name *Eskimo*, but others use only the name of their tribe. *See Author's Note, page 2.*

**fossil fuels** – natural fuels such as coal, gas, and oil, which were formed over millions of years from the remains of plankton and vegetation.

**global warming** – a rise in the overall temperature of Earth's atmosphere that threatens the environment and is caused at least in part by increased levels of greenhouse gases.

**greenhouse effect** – the trapping of Earth's heat in the lower atmosphere by greenhouse gases. The natural greenhouse effect keeps Earth warm enough to support life and does not threaten the environment.

**greenhouse gas** – a gas that slows the escape of heat from Earth into space. Most greenhouse gases are pollutants, such as carbon dioxide, ozone, methane, and nitrous oxide. Ordinary water vapor is also a powerful greenhouse gas.

**Inuit** – indigenous people of northern Canada and parts of Greenland and Alaska. *See Author's Note, page 2.*

**Iñupiaq** (plural: Iñupiat) – (1) a member of an indigenous group of Eskimos living in northwestern Alaska; (2) the language of this group; (3) descriptive word meaning "of or relating to" this group. *See Author's Note, page 2.*

**Kivgiq** – a three-day festival that honors the Iñupiaq whaling tradition.

**maktak** – Iñupiaq word for the skin and part of the blubber of a whale. It is eaten uncooked (fresh or frozen) or cooked or preserved in a variety of ways.

**North Slope** – Alaska's Tundra Region, extending north from the Brooks Range to the Arctic Ocean.

**ozone (O$_3$)** – a colorless, toxic gas with a strong odor. It is formed via electrical discharges or ultraviolet light in oxygen, and from light interacting with pollutants emitted through burning fossil fuels. High in the atmosphere, ozone blocks out harmful ultraviolet rays. At ground level, ozone acts as a greenhouse gas.

**permafrost** – in areas that are cold year round, a layer of frozen soil that lies under the top layer and stays frozen throughout the year.

**pressure ridge** – a ridge of ice, up to 100 feet (35 meters) high and sometimes several kilometers long, produced from the shear forces of moving sea ice.

**tundra** – a vast, flat, treeless Arctic region of Europe, Asia, and North America in which the subsoil is permanently frozen.

**Umialik** (plural: Umialgich) – leader of an Iñupiaq community, often a whaling captain.

**umiaq** – a traditional Iñupiaq sealskin whale-hunting boat.

# What You Can Do . . .

to fight global climate change.

Change your attitude! We can make a huge difference if everyone makes manageable changes in their lifestyle. Why should you? Because, not only is it the right thing to do, it will also save money. So, why not?

Ride less, walk more, and ride a bike. You'll save money and feel better.

Change the light bulbs in your room to compact fluorescents. Turn off your lights and computer when they are not in use.

If it's OK with your parents, set your thermostat to a lower temperature in the winter and a higher one in the summer.

Write to your power company and ask them what they are doing to increase their use of renewable energy.

Ask your representatives in the Senate and Congress what they are doing.

Plant trees—lots of them.

*For more information, go to:*

www.realclimate.org

www.purdue.edu/climate

www.climatecrisis.org

www.epa.gov/globalwarming/kids/difference.html

www.nrdc.org/globalwarming/f101.asp

www.sierraclub.org/globalwarming

# Suggested Reading

*Books*

Hess, Bill. *Gift of the Whale: The Iñupiat Bowhead Hunt, a Sacred Tradition.* Seattle: Sasquatch Books, 1999.

Revkin, Andrew C. *The North Pole Was Here: Puzzles and Perils at the Top of the World.* Boston: Kingfisher, 2006.

Wohlforth, Charles. *The Whale and the Supercomputer: On the Northern Front of Climate Change.* New York: North Point Press, 2004.

*Web Resources*

The Iñupiat Heritage Center, Barrow, Alaska
www.nps.gov/inup/siteindex.htm

Alaska Native Heritage Center
www.alaskanative.net/36.asp

Barrow Arctic Science Consortium (BASC)
www.arcticscience.org

Arctic animals site
www.arctic.noaa.gov/animals.html

All about bowhead whales
www.enchantedlearning.com/subjects/whales/species/bowheadwhale.html

Peter Lourie's Web site
www.peterlourie.com

# INDEX